WHO IS WOMAN?

How can a woman cope with a career AND
  children?
What are a woman's responsibilities in today's
  church?
Can married people have healthy friendships
  with the opposite sex?
What does the Bible say about divorce? Is it
  ever justified?

Elizabeth Skoglund's answers to these and other
questions are drawn from years of professional
counseling experience. Her aim is to restore
sanity to our lives as we understand who we
really are and how best to function—beyond
roleplay—in the world we inhabit.

WOMAN BEYOND ROLEPLAY

Elizabeth Skoglund

David C. Cook Publishing Co.

ELGIN, ILLINOIS—WESTON, ONTARIO

David C. Cook Publishing Co., Elgin, IL 60120

Printed in the United States of America
Library of Congress Catalog Number: 75-893

ISBN: 0-912692-62-6

Special acknowledgment is made to the following
for permission to reproduce extracts from copyright
material:

Harper & Row, Publishers, Inc.: *All of the Women
of the Bible*, by Edith Deen, Copyright © 1955.
Macmillan Publishing Co., Inc.: *Mere Christianity*,
by C. S. Lewis, Copyright © 1943, 1945, 1952.
The Society for Promoting Christian Knowledge:
Gold by Moonlight, Copyright © 1960 by
Christian Literature Crusade.

To my mother,
Elisabeth Benson Skoglund

FOREWORD

The very words, "women's lib," evoke strong feelings and opinions. Few contemporary subjects have generated as much heat and emotion. Consequently, to see a volume that brings light and logic to the issue from a solidly-based Biblical perspective gives me undiluted joy.

Elizabeth Skoglund speaks not just to the narrow subject of "women's lib," but to the broad issues of being a woman—a Christian woman—who must live and struggle in today's confusing social context.

Like everyone else, women are caught up in all the changes of modern life, and Ms. Skoglund suggests that today's women have one of two choices: either they can ignore the reality of what is happening all around them, pretending that change doesn't exist; or they can step out bravely and confront the tough issues that face them. There is considerable risk in both approaches. To choose the first is to risk not growing; to opt for confrontation means to run the risk of being transparent and vulnerable.

Ms. Skoglund says this whole upsetting process of sudden change is a major reason for so much of the conflict and confusion in the roles that women play today. Women play the games, often, whether they want to or not . . . the rules of which are set in cement by society, an impersonal but still powerful force that pushes modern women in a hundred directions. And like it or not, women today find that all areas of their lives are up for full review. Ms. Skoglund suggests that a Christian woman relates to this whole question differently from a non-Christian because she responds to the demands and precepts of her Christian faith—a subculture within the context of a larger culture. And her head is full of questions: Should she stay home or should she have a career? Should she have relationships with men other than her husband? If so,. what kind of relationships? If not married, what should her attitudes be toward other men? What does it mean to be feminine? How should she handle her sexual feelings? What leadership roles should she have in the church?

Ms. Skoglund is not a female chauvinist. Throughout her book she stresses the equality of man and woman. She probably will not go nearly far enough to please an active feminist, however.

There is one theme that runs throughout: Women are in no way second-rate men. They are persons first and foremost. They are also women. Ms. Skoglund encourages women to affirm that happy fact. She also hopes that women—regardless of the roles they feel they must play—will seize opportunities which are before them now to become the persons they already are, acting out with freedom their own uniqueness as persons.

Monrovia, California

W. STANLEY MOONEYHAM
PRESIDENT, WORLD
VISION INTERNATIONAL

CONTENTS

Woman As Person

JEAN CAME HOME LATER THAN USUAL that afternoon. After having lunch with her best friend, Marie, picking up the kids at Little League and Boy Scouts, and then doing the last minute grocery shopping, she barely made it home by the time her husband, Peter, walked in the door.

"Can't I ever have dinner on time these days?" he shouted at her. "Why did you have to waste time gossiping with Marie? If you had come home after work and spent the afternoon doing housework and cooking, I would have my dinner and evening's relaxation like I deserve."

Six months earlier Peter had literally dragged his twenty-eight-year-old wife to my office. "Make her more independent," he begged. "She calls me six times a day at the office, she has no friends of her own, and frankly, we could use the money if she'd get a part-time job!" I explained to Peter that if Jean's self-esteem rose sufficiently she might become independent in ways that he didn't like, as well. I stressed the value of both of them coming for counseling, rather than just Jean. But he just brushed that off, and so I had seen Jean once a week alone.

Now it was all beginning to happen. Peter was delighted with his wife's new job. Because she had more confidence he even enjoyed conversing with her more. She seemed to have opinions now and fresh ideas. Yet, she certainly wasn't there whenever he wanted her like she used to be. And he wasn't sure he liked these long lunches and especially the occasional evening out with the girls.

But if Jean was having problems, so was a close friend of hers—and Susan wasn't even married. At work her boss wanted her to bring him coffee *immediately* upon his demand. He asked her to arrange for personal gifts for his friends and family. In general, she was his girl Friday in spite of the fact that none of her male co-workers were ever asked to do these things. In her personal life Sue's boyfriend expected her to sew on his buttons and help him with certain domestic duties around his apartment. Yet when she grew tired of dating and wanted to think about marriage he reminded her that they were more liberated than that. Marriage was outdated. While he claimed to still believe in Christianity, he preferred to feel that certain teachings of Christ were not for this generation; like marriage and the protectiveness and care that a man is commanded to have toward his wife. Yet he frequently reminded her of what he called the Scriptural view of women—that of subservience to men.

America's women, married or single, are cast into a variety of roles that at times are not clearly defined and frequently conflict with each other.

As a result many married women feel put down because all they do is cook, clean house and fulfill

14

their roles as wives and mothers. And single women frequently feel inadequate because, while they may be productive in careers, they are *not* wives or mothers. So often each will say to the other "you don't know how lucky you are," because each feels like she has not risen to the expectation of what a woman ought to be in this society.

As a single person in my early twenties I remember walking into the elegantly furnished home of a good friend. Her new baby was adorable and her husband was attentive. She had all day at home and was free to go out shopping and spend her husband's money. "How ideal," I thought; for at that time I was a young teacher who had to get up early in the morning to go to work and then usually had papers to grade after school. Just as I was about to make a joking remark to that effect, Joy looked at me and said: "You're so lucky; you're free and can do something with your life." Looking at her baby with some rather deep longings of my own, I kept silent. Each of us at that time felt a sense of inadequacy and unfulfillment.

Thus whether a woman is married or single, her roles are confused. Women feel the need to excel, as do men. They study as hard in school, engage in intellectual discussions regarding issues of pertinence to our times and are in fact thinking, productive human beings. Yet how often on a date or in a marriage do women feel obligated to "act dumb" lest they threaten the male ego. Thus the same woman who effectively functions as an intelligent human being at work may pretend to be less intelligent as a wife or date. Even at work she may have to play such games as doing the work while at the same time making it look as though her boss did it.

Sometimes the conflicting demands force women into an unreal schedule of pressure and work. A housewife will try to be the perfect wife and mother and excel in a career as well. A woman who is spending a large amount of her time in her career will develop skills in cooking or sewing, even if she dislikes them, because that makes her "feel feminine."

One woman I know works full time, raises four children, bakes her own bread, plays baseball with her son, sews for her three daughters and runs the home, but goes to great pains to make it look to the outside world that it is really her husband who is the head of the home. She fulfills all of her womanly obligations as a wife and mother, then goes on to fulfill much of her husband's role because he doesn't, and then has to manipulate events so that it looks like she's just a wife and mother. She's so successful at this game playing that she even fools her own family. But she herself is an exhausted, frustrated wreck.

Part of the reason for this great confusion over the role of a woman in our society is the fast change that Americans have been undergoing. A century ago roles were clear. Women were expected to marry, bear children, please their husbands and keep house. Men were to work all day and provide food, shelter and protection for their families. Women in general were considered to be inferior in intelligence to men and certainly not as strong.

Yet through the history of mankind there have been women who rebelled at their limited position in life. A few real rebels became famous for their pre-women's lib activities. Yet there were probably hundreds or thousands of intelligent women who more quietly endured the injustice afforded them.

In the mid-seventeenth century a remarkable woman named Anne Bradstreet lived in the Massachusetts Bay Colony. It has been said that she was a very fine wife and mother, and she indicated the depth of her spiritual beliefs when she wrote:

> The world no longer let me love
> My hope and treasure lie above . . .

Yet, because she showed signs of intelligence and wrote poetry, she was scorned. In seventeenth century Massachusetts, women were not supposed to have brains. That was not part of their role. And so she writes:

> I am obnoxious to each carping tongue
> Who says my hand a needle better fits;
> A poet's pen all scorn I should thus wrong,
> For such despite they cast on female wits.

Then as a sort of compromise she continues in "The Prologue" to *The Tenth Muse Lately Sprung Up in America*:

> Men can do best, and women know it well.
> Pre-eminence in each and all is yours;
> Yet grant some small acknowledgement of ours.

Now things are different and roles are not so clearly stated as in the time of Anne Bradstreet. In her book *Woman to Woman* Eugenia Price says:

"Men have always been permitted to be people. We have just recently made it." Singleness has become acceptable to a degree, but yet for both men and women there is still the nagging notion that neither is completely where they should be in life if they are not married. Thus, although a woman in our society does not have to be married to be accepted, she will frequently feel defensive about her position. The emphasis on married groups in churches results in many single people feeling there is no place for them to fit in. Thus I have had women tell me that the main reason for their marriage is the social acceptance it brings. Yet such a basis for marriage is far from a Scriptural one when you remember that in the Bible the marriage union is compared to the love relationship that exists between Christ and His Church.

Thus change is a major reason for the conflict in women's roles. Unconscious attitudes and societal ideals conflict. It's all right to be single, but it's not all right. You should be a gourmet cook, but if you're liberated you'll use TV dinners. You should enjoy sex, but you shouldn't be the aggressor. And on and on, an endless list of paradoxical ideas could be listed which women attempt to fit into.

At two opposite ends of the spectrum are the women who avoid the conflict, choose one role and forget the rest. But one senses that they, above all, are frustrated. One patient of mine was "completely liberated." She and her husband engaged in mate swapping and in most areas of their lives they were "equal." Yet she came to me because she was a scared, disillusioned woman who was tired of a relationship which cast her into the role of being like

18

a man in every way except sexually. And even sexually she was dissatisfied because underneath she really wanted her husband for herself.

At the other extreme, a woman in her late forties was very disturbed because she was nothing but cook, maid and sex partner with a man who demanded that she be within his call every minute of the day.

Neither of these women tried to fit into the variety of roles that are open to women in this society, but neither of them were happy in their acceptance of the extreme.

Even in Christian circles the role of a woman is not clearly defined and is often contradictory. I shall never forget a woman missionary who achieved rather great acclaim in this country shouting out the words, "Where are the men?" She was specifically referring to the small mission station in interior China where she had worked for years without seeing a single male missionary. Why was it, she asked, that in America the male church-goer is usually the one who takes positions of authority in the church. Women have other functions, like cooking, Sunday school teaching and child care. But no one in the home office objected to her being pastor, deacon or elder in China, to say nothing of the back-breaking physical work which she did.

Within the Christian church there is great variety regarding women's roles. Certain denominations now ordain women as ministers, while still others do not allow women to even speak or pray in a church meeting (although I have never been able to figure out why they are still allowed to sing solos). In between these two extremes there is every variation imaginable; a woman can teach but not be a pastor, or she can pray but not teach, or she can pray if she wears a head covering.

Such disagreement and contradiction is evident in even some of the better Christian literature available on the subject, which only further illustrates the validity of such an observation.

Larry Christenson, in his book *The Christian Family,* contradicts himself, in my opinion. In speaking of the added responsibilities of women as a result of their "emancipation" he says, "all of this is contrary to Divine Order. A woman is not normally equipped by nature to sustain this kind of psychological emotional pressure and still fulfill her God-appointed role as wife and mother." Later, however, he comments: "God has given to women great talents and abilities. Their intelligence is equal to man, their stamina and emotional endurance often greater." While other parts of his book seem excellent, I was not sure what he really was saying about women.

It is my belief that the Scriptural view of a woman's role is clear and is in no way degrading. Contrary to the view that a woman is some kind of a second-rate man, the Bible presents a very high view of woman. Building upon this viewpoint it is possible for the Christian woman, even in twentieth century America, to find a role in which she is equal to man but very different from him. For God's ideal of womanhood is not degrading, nor is it definable as a cheap imitation of manhood. To Him she is a unique individual with capacities which have too long been denied or made light of.

Woman in Culture

JENNIFER HAD RECENTLY BECOME ENGAGED to a man whom her family had known before either of them entered first grade. Yet she felt uneasy about the arrangement. Seven months earlier she had broken off a relationship with a man whom she had loved very deeply but who did not share her religious beliefs. Yet this time things weren't right either. Ed was a fine man: spiritual, conscientious, bright, handsome. Still, the love she had previously experienced did not exist toward Ed as far as Jennifer was concerned. She admired Ed, but in spite of his love for her she could not return his love in the same way.

Confused, she turned to a girl friend whom she had met in college. Kimberly was Chinese and had been brought up in Formosa. Because Jennifer's family was promoting the marriage, she hoped to find some kind of objective viewpoint in Kim.

To her surprise Kim didn't understand at all! The love of the man, not that of the woman, was the important thing according to Kim. What was vital was the couple's compatibility and the family approval, both of which were abundantly present. Two cultures had met and clashed over the issue of marriage. To Jennifer a feeling of romantic love was of paramount importance. To Kim a woman's love would be developed slowly in a good marriage, while family approval was of greater importance.

Many of us grow up feeling that our image of a woman and her role is an innate, inborn thing. Actually the opposite is closer to the truth. While men and women are certainly different in physical-biochemical ways, much of what each develops into and defines as masculine or feminine, in both dress and behavior, depends upon the prevailing culture.

Mayan women, for example, dressed far less elaborately than men. They wore essentially no clothing above the waist and their skirts came below the knee. They were very retiring and did not meet with men in public at all. Indian women living in the same geographical area today dress in much the same way.

Their male counterparts, however, wore elaborate costumes to the point of even dressing up as various animals. Of primary importance were their elaborate headdresses, which usually contained flowers or feathers.

Indeed, until the nineteenth century men tended to be dressed in elaborate finery, as in most cases women were too. In early Babylonian times men and women both wore their hair equally long. Both wore their hair up on their heads, although women arranged theirs more elaborately. In Greece short hair did not become acceptable until the fifth century.

In many early cultures jewelry was worn by both men and women. And up until the time of the Norman Conquest trousers were considered barbarian.

While most cultures have imposed a male-dominant role on women, in some places that has been minimized and perhaps even become nonexistent. When Elisabeth Elliot first went to live with the very primitive Auca Indians she found that women held their own with their husbands and refused to obey commands with impunity.

Of dubious veracity but of considerable interest is the legend of the Amazon women. As legend has it the Amazons had their own culture with no men allowed. They were a powerful group of women who once a year would leave their tribe, seek out a man, and bear his child. The man was not allowed back into the village with them and if the child was a boy he was destroyed at birth.

What we do know, however, apart from legend, is that some Amazon women were captured and enslaved. A certain number were made into warriors, and according to accurate historical records, they fought well and were admired for their endurance.

One could pursue endlessly the cultural mold that women have created or fit into in various societies. However, whatever the culture, the expectations of its women seem to have been moderately clear-cut. This is not true of our American culture today and that is partially why women are frustrated by the numerous and often contradictory demands which are made upon them.

For the Christian the confusion must be resolved somewhat differently than for the non-Christian. Christianity is a subculture within a much larger culture. As such it does not just provide spiritual life for its believers but it dictates a very definite culture within which a woman's role is defined. That role is wisely defined in a fairly general way so that a woman will blend somewhat into the culture in which

25

she lives. For example, nowhere in the Bible is a woman told how long to wear her skirts. That is left to the definition of modesty which exists in the broader culture in which she lives. In 1955 it would have been immodest in this culture to wear skirts above the knee. In 1970 this was acceptable—at least for most of us!

Thus there are some general principles which apply to the Christian woman and provide the divinely appointed cultural guide for her. These general principles will be discussed here, with later chapters considering specific areas—for example, sex, divorce or the local church.

One of the characteristics most often repeated in the Bible which is to be found in a Christian woman is that of modesty. Because it has been talked about so much the word has almost lost any valid meaning. In my mind, at least, it conjures up a sort of meek, mousy person who is completely unsure of herself and utterly dowdy and unattractive.

As a child I can remember seeing a picture in an antique shop of a lovely old-fashioned lady sitting in front of a large mirror powdering her face. Then as the picture was looked at from a different angle, the lady's reflection in the mirror became a skull. That, I was taught, was the result of vanity, of not being modest. That image, too, comes to my mind as I think of the word modesty.

Christians have not only distorted and exaggerated the meaning of modesty, but they are at times contradictory about the whole thing. A church group recently scheduled a convention in a hot, dry city which was far from any lake or the ocean. Eyebrows were raised when I jokingly said, "Why don't you go to the beach where you can get a tan in your spare time?" They *purposely* chose that remote, dry city so that the young people would not be "tempted to indulge in mixed bathing." The inconsistency lies here: in that same church a number of women of all ages wear dresses which are cut far too low to be decent for daytime wear. Why worry about the beach if you're going to look seductive at church?

What then is modesty? Modesty in clothing means a lack of extravagance, gaudiness, seductiveness. Clothes can be extremely provocative through suggesting nudity. A Christian woman should look fashionable and appealing, but clothing which brings undue attention to a woman's body is not modest. And any woman knows when she's wearing something like that!

What is modest in clothing varies from place to place and time to time. A bathing suit can be modest on the beach but not modest on the streets of New York City. A woman may wear a lower cut dress at an evening party than she can comfortably wear at her place of business. Short skirts may be acceptable in America and not in New Zealand.

But within the boundaries of modesty a woman will like herself better and be more attractive to others if she dresses with taste and some awareness of current fashion. I remember one Sunday school teacher I had who dressed terribly. Everything about her was plain. Her dresses were long. Her hair was pulled back into a little knot. It was very difficult for teenagers to be interested in the Christianity she taught because her appearance was such a hindrance. She actually called attention to herself in the name of modesty.

Not long ago a teenage girl was dragged in to see me because her parents were afraid she would run away. Long ago she had turned off to Christianity. Before she came, her parents made the unfortunate mistake of telling her I was a good Christian and would help her. I don't know exactly what she expected but after she had been in my office for a few minutes she began to relax and said: "You don't look like I expected you to look." Drab, old-maidish looking clothes could have really alienated her.

As a teenager I went to a very strict Christian school where makeup was considered sinful and everyone looked pretty drab. When I freed myself from those legalistic rules and began to enjoy make-up and color and relatively up-to-date clothes, I enjoyed my femininity a lot more. And I found it helped me reach out to many more people.

But a woman is not just modest in the clothes she wears. Modesty also relates to speech. Again some of this has to do with the times in which we live. Certain words can be used by women today which would have shocked our grandparents. But coarseness is still something which a Christian woman should avoid.

What is modest or immodest about a conversation depends a great deal upon the setting. What I can tell my doctor might be immodest to tell a dinner guest. What my patients talk about openly in my office might be inappropriate to tell some friends.

Yet I believe that, in general, Christians need to loosen up in their ability to express their feelings. For example, modesty demands that you not discuss your sex life freely at a dinner party. Some people may, but it seems unwise for a variety of reasons.

But every woman should feel free to discuss anything that bothers her with *someone*. The problem is to find the right person and the right time.

A Christian woman recently came to me professionally to discuss masturbation. As a child she had been warned that if she engaged in this she would lose her mind. By the time she reached me she was really panicked and yet almost unable to talk about it. Talking about this in public could probably be considered immodest. But certainly in all these years she should have been able to find some person to whom she could have talked—and that would not have been immodest. If we Christians were a little more Christlike, people wouldn't always have to go to a professional counselor in order to feel safe and accepted in the discussion of such topics. A woman who accepts herself will follow appropriate social rules in general conversation but will also be able to comfortably discuss more intimate problems with other people when the need arises. Prudishness is not modesty. Good taste is.

C. S. Lewis sums up the idea of modesty well in his book *Mere Christianity* where he says:

> The Christian rule of chastity must not be confused with the social rule of 'modesty' . . . The social rule of propriety lays down how much of the human body should be displayed and what subjects can be referred to, and in what words, according to the customs of a given social circle. Thus, while the rule of chastity is the same for all Christians at all times, the rule of propriety changes. A girl in the Pacific Islands wearing hardly any clothes and a Victo-

rian lady completely covered in clothes might both be equally "modest," proper, or decent, according to the standards of their own societies; and both, for all we could tell by their dress, might be equally chaste (or equally unchaste). Some of the language which chaste women used in Shakespeare's time would have been used in the nineteenth century only by a woman completely abandoned . . . .

In I Timothy 2, in addition to modesty a woman is to be characterized by good works. The two qualities are not disconnected, for in between the two, hairstyles and jewelry are mentioned, which Paul is not condemning. Rather he is saying that the outstanding qualities which people should notice in a woman are her modesty and good works. Again, too many Christians have distorted these verses and made an issue out of wearing jewelry, for example.

In I Timothy 5: 10 (The Living Bible) these good works are defined. In these verses Paul is giving a special role to older widows and one of the qualifications is that they must have performed good works as younger women. Then these good works are listed:

Has she brought up her children well? Has she been kind to strangers as well as to other Christians? Has she helped those who are sick and hurt? Is she always ready to show kindness?

Most of the major women in the Bible were very hospitable and so this, combined with the above verse, seems a part of the role of a Christian woman.

The hospitality referred to here is not part of an ingroup, how-can-I-outdo-the-last-person, type of entertaining. When I was in college I occasionally went to San Diego for a variety of reasons. One widow who belonged to my church denomination there hardly knew me, but insisted that I always stay with her. She did this for a number of people. She knew how to practice hospitality.

Another woman is constantly having someone for dinner who needs to get away for a while—or for the weekend if that's what will help most. Her phone, too, is busy, not with gossips but with people who know they can turn to her. Yet here I must interject an additional point. Her life is not just one big job of cooking, washing and answering the phone. She is a talented musician, a Bible teacher, and a woman who has the intellect to be a compatible wife for a well-trained, intelligent husband.

Good works? The list is endless. They may be as simple as cooking a meal or as complicated as building a hospital. The key thought in the above verse in Timothy seems to be the last sentence: "Is she always ready to show kindness?" Love doesn't say, "I'll feed you if you become a Christian" or "if you stop living the way you do."

I know one woman who in what *she* thinks is love went to visit a very sick, frightened teenage girl and told her that Satan was in her making her sick. Such was not the case at all and her visit did not show kindness; it showed a hard, rigid inflexibility which is not God's idea of a woman.

The Christian woman will undoubtedly want to adopt many of the characteristics of the society in which she lives: the greater individuality which a woman today enjoys, broader job choices and educational possibilities, a greater variety of styles in clothing and so on. When these do not conflict with her Christian beliefs a woman *should* blend into the greater culture. But added to these are the two additional Christian values of modesty and good works.

I used to hear it said that Christians should be known because they are different—and different seemed to mean odd, outdated—in general, a little out of it. I say a Christian woman should stand out because she shows so much love and acceptance to those around her and uses her talents and intelligence so thoroughly that people admire her and are drawn to her.

Woman As Partner

NANCY WAS IN HER THIRTIES when I first met her. She was attractive in a remote way that made one feel that most of her beauty was in the past, as was her freedom and ambition.

She had one small child upon whom she lavished all of her time and attention, except, of course, when her husband Scott was home. Then she brought him whatever he needed, cooked all the foods he liked, ran his errands, and at the end of such a day wearily tried to be an interested sex partner. She had no identity of her own, not really even with Scott. She was in some ways just a convenience, almost a commodity to be used.

Phyllis was completely the opposite. She and her husband Darrell had their equality worked out to a science. They both worked; they both divided *all* housework down the middle. And each spent his own money. The trouble is, they spent a lot of time just figuring out what was the other person's fair share of responsibility. For them, too, love seemed secondary at best, and at times there seemed to be no love at all. Phyllis was so concerned about being liberated and Darrell so anxious not to appear outdated in his viewpoints that their whole relationship was a series of arguments, each afraid to really give to the other.

Both of these illustrations are somewhat extreme and yet they represent two conflicting views of marriage which exist in our society. And in reality there are marriages that go to greater extremes than these: a wife who cannot go to a neighbor's house without permission from her husband; a woman who says, "I don't have to learn to cook, I'll just make my husband do that"—and he does; a wife who talks her husband into having sex with her best friend so that she can feel more free to sleep with her friend's husband.

The Biblical view of a woman's role in marriage is perhaps most clearly stated in Ephesians 5: 22, 23 (Phillips): "You wives must learn to adapt yourselves to your husbands, as you submit yourselves to the Lord, for the husband is the 'head' of the wife in the same way that Christ is head of the Church. . . ."

However, in I Corinthians 11: 11, 12 (Amplified) Paul says: "Nevertheless, in [the plan of] the Lord and from His point of view woman is not apart from and independent of man, nor is man aloof from and independent of woman; For as woman was made from man, even so man is also born of woman. And all [whether male or female go forth] from God (as their Author)."

Thus there is a complementary function of the husband to that of the role of the wife. Reading on in Ephesians, the fifth chapter (Phillips), Paul says: "The husband must give his wife the same sort of love that Christ gave to the Church, when he sacrificed himself for her."

Women are equal to men as people with intelligence and talent—as people of worth. Before God a person's sex does not make him either superior or inferior; for before God there is neither male nor female. Yet as far as roles are concerned, the role of a Christian wife is to be under the authority of her husband, while his role is to love her with the same kind of love Christ showed when He died on the cross. When a wife fails in her role, she ends up in a taking position with a husband who loves her—and makes it hard for him to maintain that love. When a man fails in his role, a wife lives under a kind of tyranny; for authority without love results in tyranny.

If both the husband and wife fulfill their roles, the two meet in the middle and each extends himself for the other. This principle may be seen in a small matter such as the giving of a dinner party. Jean wanted to have some guests for dinner on a Friday night. While her husband Mike could have managed it that night, Friday was a demanding day for him, so he asked Jean to invite their friends for Saturday. While her preference was Friday, she agreed and went ahead with her plans for Saturday. Jean could have made a big point about equal rights. On the other hand, Mike didn't ask her to change in order to flaunt his authority. He made a reasonable request— and out of love he didn't demand, he requested. More than that, when Saturday came Jean didn't even need to argue her rights in expecting Mike to help her, especially since it was his day off. Out of love he helped without being asked.

Jean wasn't tyrannized, but she adapted to Mike's needs. Each felt the other's love because each extended himself for the other.

If childhood is the time when individuals first learn to evaluate their worth, then marriage is the time of life that for most people either improves or helps destroy their self-esteem. A woman who is tyrannized cannot help but feel put down. A man who is dominated by a castrating female will feel equally put down. The Biblical roles for a marriage relationship can be very effective in building good self-esteem if both partners adhere to them.

Idealistic? Perhaps. Yet possible too since God does not dangle idealism tantalizingly in front of our faces, knowing all along that it can never be ours. Yet, realistically, no marriage maintains such a relationship at all times. To varying degrees each or both of the marriage partners fall short. Still, if one is able to maintain his or her role when the other slips, that positive action will often cause positive behavior on the part of the other which will in turn elevate this feeling of self-esteem in both.

For example, Beth clearly did not want Chuck to play tennis more than once a week. Between the tennis and the nights late at the office, she felt that she saw little enough of him. Chuck, on the other hand, was getting tired of being nagged about the use of his time. The more Beth complained, the later Chuck stayed out. Beth had become an unhappy, dominating wife, and Chuck was anything but considerate and loving. Then one night when Chuck walked angrily out of the house to go to a friend's Beth suddenly realized what was happening. After waiting for him to arrive at his friend's house, Beth called. "I'm taking the children out for ice cream," she said in a pleasant voice. "I didn't want you to worry. Have a good time."

Next week when Chuck saw me his first question was, "Did you tell her to call me?" I was glad I could answer, "No." Not only had Beth's phone call literally made Chuck's whole evening, but the next night he stayed home because he preferred her company, now that she was pleasant; and he began to realize that he, too, had not been considering his wife's needs. Both were happier; both treated each other better; and each felt a greater sense of worth because each was behaving in a more responsible way. They liked each other and themselves better.

Negative action does indeed create a negative response. A woman who commands her husband to help her with the dishes may receive a very unloving response. On the other hand the woman who says, "I know we're both tired at the end of a rough day, but would you mind helping me with dinner so that we can get through and relax?" is more likely to meet with a favorable response. Indeed such consideration is neither more nor less than we should use in our dealings with all people. It certainly does not imply a sickening, subservient attitude on the part of a wife toward her husband.

For example, in a book called *Fascinating Womanhood* by Helen B. Andelin, the woman's role in my opinion, becomes nauseating—and destructive. With very distorted Biblical interpretation, using the verse, "Except ye become as a little child, ye shall not enter into the Kingdom of Heaven," Mrs. Andelin suggests that a wife should learn to "release unhappy emotions through childlikeness." And what does a child do when she becomes angry? ". . . she stamps her foot and shakes her curls and pouts. She gets adorably angry . . . finally she switches off and

39

threatens never to speak to you again." Says Mrs. Andelin, "childlike anger will not annoy a man, but will rather amuse him." Furthermore, says Mrs. Andelin, an "able, intellectual and competent woman" will only threaten a man. That, to me, is not only a put-down on women but a degrading statement about men. The men I respect would detest a woman who stamped her foot and pouted, and would be fascinated, to use Mrs. Andelin's word, by a woman with ability and potential as long as with those qualities she was also feminine.

But then Mrs. Andelin's overall definition of femininity also seems a little strange to me. She even carries the concept of childlikeness into the area of clothing: She says women should visit a child's dress store, look up children's sewing patterns and emulate these in their dress. They shouldn't wear tailored clothes and should avoid to some degree the use of high heels; while they are feminine they are not childlike. And as far as feminine tasks are concerned, she says that earning money, handling money, traveling alone across country and doing household tasks like painting are simply not to be done.

To take the time to go into these unscriptural ideas is annoying because they seem so obviously inaccurate. I can't think of many more effective ways for a woman to turn off a man who has any ego strength at all. Furthermore, there are few ways I can think of that would better destroy a woman's chances of survival in a divorce or widowhood. And I cannot escape my curiosity about her opinion of the very feminine yet hard-working women who bore men's burdens in the founding of this country—including Mormon women of which she is one.

Yet many women I encounter have read this book and for many men and women alike it has been a source of some confusion over roles within their marriages.

Other books and courses currently being offered to the American church woman are equally confusing. One well known book and course seems to me to present two grave errors of teaching. In the first place, there appears to almost be a deification of the male. Rather than an emphasis on the mutual re-responsibilities of marriage, the man is made into a small god. Also, while the acceptance of sex as good and healthy is great, one comes away with the idea of a worldly seductiveness. The real meaning of sex in a Christian sense seems obliterated by a shallow cheapness which uses the technique of a prostitute— and a rather desperate one at that!

Marriage is a matter of give and take, of extending oneself beyond the boundaries of "what he deserves," or "what my rights are." But there is a fine line which some cross which puts a woman in a position of being walked over. That is not Scriptural. Nor is a role of childlikeness and soap-opera helplessness Biblical.

Part of extending oneself for the other, means *hearing* what they say. Not long ago in my office a man said of his wife, "I love her." Five minutes later she said to me, "If John would only *say* he loved me." Barbara, on the other hand, said in his presence, "I wish I had some time to be alone." Just a few minutes later John said, "I'd like to have the time to go bowling but Barbara wants me with her all the time." As they talked, each time they tuned each other out I stopped them and forced them to listen.

41

After a few sessions they knew some needs that the other had in a way that had never occurred to them before. Sometimes in a marriage two people become frustrated just because they never stop long enough to really hear what the other is saying. And this is true of parents and children too.

The principle of reaching out to build up the other is of paramount importance in the sexual realm. As a negative example, in *Mein Kampf* Adolf Hitler adopts a very materialistic viewpoint regarding sex in marriage. Says Hitler, "Not even marriage can be an end in itself; it must serve the greater purpose of increasing and preserving species and race. That alone is its meaning and its purpose."

Sexual feelings are apparently meant to be enjoyed since they have been given by God in such great intensity. Rather than being given simply for the propagation of the race, the sexual union is the highest expression of love between two people and is compared to Christ's love for the Church. As such it should hardly be considered dirty. Yet so often dirty is the way it comes through to a child. I watched one child ask his grandfather a question about a verse in the Bible which related to the pregnancy of a woman. Everyone grew suddenly quiet and disapproving and the child was told to "ask his mother." Thoroughly confused and shamed, I doubt he went on to ask anyone. Who'd take that chance a second time!

Furthermore, sex is meant to be an act of giving as well as receiving. As such it should be enjoyed by both husband and wife. Another myth about sex that is still with us is that sex is meant for male and not female enjoyment. One woman told me how she "endures" sex because her husband wants it. Another woman who was in a position of leadership with Christian girls told them that when they married they would have to "put up with sex" because the man deserved it. This is not scriptural.

However, at the other extreme is the idea that in every sex relationship both husband and wife are equally fulfilled. A person's sexual response may vary according to a fluctuating hormone balance, fatigue, pressure, work and a myriad of other factors. In no way can the response of either person be the same from one time to another. At times there will be little or no response, but some opportune emotional support may help prevent the condition from becoming chronic.

A tired, overworked businessman who becomes temporarily impotent should not be put down by his wife. Her support and understanding will help him to more quickly respond in the future. Likewise, a wife who is experiencing anxiety over a sick child or a teenager involved in drugs may find herself frigid. An understanding husband will realize the underlying reasons and by his reassurance probably help her avoid a prolonged period of sexual withdrawal.

If sexual problems occur with either mate there are times when professional attention may help and no one should feel reticent about seeking that help. More often, perhaps, the encouragement, respect and love that comes from a husband or wife who really understands and is not threatened by the situation will be the best therapy. For fear of sexual failure or a compulsion to succeed may inhibit a person's sexual capability.

This concept is substantiated by psychiatrist Viktor Frankl when he says: "Something goes wrong when the consciousness attempts to regulate acts which normally take place, so to speak, without thought. . . . Fear of sleeplessness is an anticipating anxiety which in such cases hinders falling asleep, thus confirming the fact of insomnia, which in turn reinforces the anticipatory anxiety—a vicious circle.

"A similar process takes place in all persons who have become insecure sexually. Their self observation is sharpened and they start out with the fear of not succeeding. This anxiety leads itself to sexual failure. The sexual neurotic no longer fixes his mind upon his partner (as does the lover), but upon the sexual act as such. Consequently the act fails, must fail, because it does not take place 'simply,' is not performed naturally, but is willed."

At this point it is perhaps important to point out that in twentieth century America we have cheapened the concept of sex by placing an all-important value on it. For, again according to Viktor Frankl, sex "is not an end in itself, but a means of expression. Love as such can exist without it. Where sexuality is possible, love will desire and seek it; but where renunciation is called for, love will not necessarily cool or die." Sex is probably one of the greatest sources of enjoyment that God has given to men and women, yet it is not a commodity—nor is a woman a commodity. Sex is an expression of love.

While both husband and wife are meant to enjoy the sexual relationship, women have different needs than men. For men a quick, immediate response is frequently sufficient. Women more often need a man to be gentle and slow, both in the buildup to intercourse and in intercourse itself. She needs fondling and verbal expressions of love in addition to intercourse. She needs to feel loved, not used. If a man is really fulfilling the role of loving his wife, he will pay attention to these needs.

Above all, anything is sacred in the marriage bed. There is no such thing as sexual perversion between two reasonably normal married people. The main issue is whether or not both are comfortable with their sexual activity and agree upon it. No one should ever be forced to engage in sexual activity which offends. On the other hand if two married people agree about their sexual relationship and feel comfortable with it they should not feel the need to continually analyze it for its normalcy. In a sense, sexual behavior is a very creative thing between two people and they should be free to use that creativity without guilt as long as it, again, builds up the other.

Within the marriage bond there should be two equal people fulfilling two God-appointed roles which mutually build them into people with a greater sense of worth. But marriage can potentially be one of the most destructive experiences available.

A couple I know have demonstrated to me the possibilities inherent in a marriage which fulfills God's purposes. They never really demand anything of each other, yet each gives constantly. Neither distrusts the other and their trust breeds trust. They never force each other to tell them where the other went or who they saw or why they're late. Yet each wants to tell these things and does. In a sense the whole relationship was summed up at a time when the husband received a high award of achievement. When his wife looked at him proudly and said, "You've done a wonderful job," he looked back at her and replied, "You're more than half of it."

Woman As Friend

CLARK AND I BECAME deeply engrossed as we explored the possibilities for helping teenagers on drugs. Clark's wife, Edith, had been as involved as we, until the phone rang and she was trapped for a good forty-five minutes.

Now as she filled our coffee cups for the fifth time and re-joined us, she too became involved again. Ideas seemed to flow as the hours went by: ideas on drug rehabilitation; thoughts for a new book; even an exciting idea for making educational cassettes. But more than that, we were close and united in our thoughts and feelings. Suddenly I looked at the clock: Two a.m.! Since I had to get up early the next morning, I hurriedly got up to leave. We had been brain-storming for six hours—and to each of us it had seemed like two.

On the way home I thought about the great relationship the three of us had. And the friendship was just as close with Clark as with Edith.

A friend once said to me: "I don't believe a woman can have a friendship with a man other than her husband. It always becomes too involved." Yet it is hard for me to feel that a woman's role in friendship should be restricted to her husband, if she has one, and her female friends.

To the contrary, while there are potential problems inherent in relationships between women and men to whom they are not married, such relationships can be healthy and vital. Furthermore no woman, married or single, can avoid these relationships entirely. They will occur if a woman is in the business world in almost any capacity. They are present in the activities that couples engage in. And for the woman who is widowed, divorced or single they are important in a well rounded social life. Few women enjoy the exclusive company of women only.

When I was teaching tenth graders in high school I often overheard teenagers giggle when the word love was mentioned because they always associated love with sex—usually forbidden sex. Embarrassment and confusion regarding the word love is not just a teenage peculiarity. It carries over into adulthood. I recently watched several adults playing a game which, if you arrive at a certain space, requires that you tell someone you love them if you have not already used that word during the day. A bit silly? Perhaps. But certainly not life threatening—and that is exactly the way most people responded. Some refused to say it; one clenched his hands, looked upward at the ceiling and choked out the words!

Love is a feeling of closeness toward someone, a sense of warmth, a desire to enjoy that person's company. Certainly this at times includes sexual attraction toward someone of the opposite sex, but it does not preclude a relationship with the opposite sex which may not involve romantic attachment. Love is not synonymous with sex. It is not always easy to keep out the romantic element but it is possible. Grasping this concept will perhaps free some women to increase the breadth of their relationships; for it is possible and healthy for men and women to have meaningful relationships apart from sexual attraction. Thus a married woman may find a friend in a married man, or a single woman in a married man, without adversely affecting their marriage.

One woman I know has no male friends except her husband. Oh, she knows a few men but there is no real relationship involved. She has bluntly verbalized a deep fear of being close to a man because "friendships with men don't work."

In a school where I once taught there were several married men, an unmarried woman and myself who became good friends. We had parties on people's birthdays and used to get into long philosophical debates during lunch. These were honest discussions involving school problems, how we felt about our goals in life, and even personal needs. Sometimes someone would have a particular problem, like the day that one member of the group had to put an elderly relative in a convalescent home, and we would try to give that person some support. At the time I was deeply involved in working with a large number of students on drugs, which was a very demanding job. I can't count the times that one of those men would come and drag me away for lunch because they knew I needed the break, or the times they covered for me in a class so that I could finish talking to an individual student who needed me. That was love—but not romantic love, for none of us was *in* love with any of the others. In fact, some of the happiest times we had were at Christmas when we would get together for dinner and include dates and wives. We were all just close friends and to a degree we will always be so.

For me, as a single woman, the closeness of a group that included both men and women was important. Previously I had taught in a girls' school where the exclusive company of only females lacked something. As an unmarried woman my needs include male relationships. Sometimes that means I get hurt, because I start to feel something deeper than friendship toward someone who can't return that feeling. But I have found that such feelings can be controlled a great deal more completely than most of us admit. At times, too, someone feels deeply toward me and I am unable to return the feelings and allow the relationship to deepen, either because he is already married or because for a variety of reasons I do not feel we are suited for each other. Thus risk and hurt are part of life if one is truly alive; and without them one lives an isolated, safe existence where the risk is minimal—but so is the joy and fulfillment.

Married women, too, profit from male as well as female relationships. One woman I know has an interesting, attentive husband. They share their feelings and have many common interests. Yet regarding a philanthropic project of hers, she can evoke little interest from him. Another friend and his wife spend a good deal of time talking with her and giving her suggestions in this area, and this way she gets a male as well as a female viewpoint. Both couples are good friends and there is no jealousy.

Women in this culture are conditioned to feel that there is strength in male support during a crisis and that a male viewpoint on business affairs is often more objective and knowledgeable. For whatever the reason, these feelings seem to prevail. Immediately following the death of my baby nephew, which hit me harder than anyone in my family knew, a male friend of mine took me from the hospital to the beach for dinner. At that point I wanted him, not a girl friend. More recently, during my father's terminal illness, I needed different kinds of support: the luncheon chats with a close girl friend; the valuable before-I-went-to-bed telephone calls from another close female friend; the male friend who went with me into that bleak intensive care unit and held my hand tightly while he prayed; and the variety of people, male and female, who were always available and caring.

When my father was alive, it was his advice I wanted on financial matters, not my mother's. Even now there are a couple of male friends to whom I turn when I need business advice; and even when my female friends say almost the same things, I tend to believe the men more. I'm not saying this is logical—but it's the way many women feel. I'm sure that men, too, feel that they get a certain different meeting of needs from female relationships. And, once again, I am not writing here of anything romantic or sexual—just the personality differences that exist between men and women and how those differences make for a variety in friendship. True, many of these differences are probably cultural and these statements should not be construed as a put-down on women. But like it or not, they exist. And while I am fully in support of woman's equality in ability, payment for jobs, and other rights I would not enjoy living in a culture where I was the same as a man. I like to have a man open a door for me and buy me a cup of coffee. I enjoy looking different than a man. But I don't enjoy being walked over or ignored because I'm a woman. Women are different from men—and both men and women should enjoy these differences —but women are not less valuable than men. Upon this premise lies the basis for a good relationship between a man and woman.

Repeatedly in the New Testament Paul refers to the women who worked with him. They were not merely business colleagues, for he often stayed in their homes and they nursed him through several illnesses. Yet Paul was single, at least during part of this time, and many of these women were married. Therefore, from a Scriptural point of view there seems to be the attitude that men and women can be close friends apart from any romantic involvement.

For the woman who chooses to have good friendships with men, apart from marriage, there are certain moral obligations. It is important to appear right before the world around you, even when you yourself know that everything is right. This fits into Paul's admonition not to cause your brother to stumble and to avoid the stigma of evil. And it is vital that in relating to a married man you scrupulously avoid behavior that could hurt his marriage.

For example, I have a friendship with a couple who are about the same age as I am. Jeannette took her three children and went away for the weekend to visit her mother. Joe was left home alone. Lonely, he called and asked me out for dinner. Jeannette knew and approved; Joe and I were friends but no more. Yet what was right between us was still not a good

54

idea. For one reason, others seeing us would have possibly put a different meaning into it—particularly since we would have had to go out in the evening when it would look more social than professional. Furthermore, with Joe, people already knew we were friends, not just business associates. And to top it all off, Joe and Jeannette were not getting along too well at the time, which gave me my most important reason for saying, "No."

Sex too may become an issue at times if a woman and man become friends. Even if the woman and man are both single a sexual relationship is not acceptable by Scriptural standards. Biblically the sex act epitomizes the highest expression of love within a marriage and is paralleled with the union of Christ and His Church. It is, therefore, not an act which should be lightly engaged in because of the physical and even emotional desires of a night out. It is here that the single woman may have a greater problem than the married woman, for the married woman is presumably having her sexual needs met by her husband. But for the single woman, or the married woman who is having marital difficulties, sexual needs may at times be great.

Even apart from Christianity, sex outside of marriage is not a completely satisfactory answer. Many women interpret intercourse as an act which means a permanent relationship. When it does not prove to be more than a short range affair a woman may feel deeply rejected and unlovable. For the Christian woman there are the added problems of guilt and feelings of spiritual alienation from both Christian friends and God. One woman I know who has been sexually involved with a married man has given up all her Christian friends because she can't face them. Another can't feel free in her devotional life with God because she is in direct conflict with His will. Any of the women I have talked to who are having premarital or extramarital affairs and who are evangelical in their beliefs seem to live lives of carefully contrived secrecy which are not conducive to good mental health.

Yet women who have no sexual outlet still have God-given sexual needs. Busyness, helping others, creative activities may help but they are far from complete answers. Knowing that these needs are real and right and certainly nothing to be ashamed of helps too. No woman should feel guilty over having healthy sexual drives. The married woman who said to me, "Sex is something women have to endure," was not expressing a healthy viewpoint but rather a very repressive attitude. In contrast, a woman who accepts her femininity and has access to her feelings will feel sexual needs which will be present even when there is no desire to have children.

While some Christians are strongly opposed to the idea of sexual fantasies, others feel that at times they may be a partial answer for those who have no sexual outlet. The following verse may be a problem to those who do have fantasies but feel guilt about them. "Anyone who even looks at a woman with lust in his eye has already committed adultery with her in his heart" (Mt. 5: 28, The Living Bible). But in speaking of this text, Paul Tournier, M.D., says of a single man who felt guilt over his imagination: "I have pointed out to him the obvious fact that this text did not apply to him, since he was a bachelor, or at least did not apply to him unless his glance led him to covet a woman he knew to be married."

Furthermore in considering the text in Matthew the interpretation of the word "lust" seems pivotal. The same Greek word is translated desire, covet, and lust throughout the New Testament and its meaning is not automatically one of sinfulness, nor does it always relate to sex. Rather, according to James Strong in his *Concordance* the word means "to set the heart upon, long for." In *A New and Concise Bible Dictionary* it is translated "to desire earnestly."

In Matthew 13: 17 (TLB) Christ says: "Many a prophet and godly man has longed to see what you have seen . . ." In I Timothy 3: 1 Paul says: " . . . If a man desire the office of a bishop, he *desireth* a good work." Galatians 5: 17 reads: "For the flesh *lusteth* against the Spirit, and the Spirit against the flesh. . . . " And again in Acts 20: 33 Paul says: "I have *coveted* no man's silver, or gold, or apparel." All these verses use the same Greek word as is used in Matthew 5: 28. None of them have sexual references and all indicate strong desire to the point of action. For example when Paul speaks in Acts about not coveting their gold, I'm sure he's not saying he wouldn't *like* it; he is saying something much stronger, that he doesn't covet it, wish for it to the point of dwelling on it in his thoughts and perhaps stealing it. Thus when Christ speaks of lusting after a woman, the thought is not so much of a passing sexual fantasy but something stronger.

The rightness and wrongness of sexual fantasies have been the subject of some controversy and for each individual a decision must ultimately be made between himself and God. No one should legislate rules for the consciences of others to the degree that even their thought life is totally under the control of someone else's conscience. In the Christian world alone you will find opinions ranging from "allow your imagination to go in any direction you want" to "all daydreaming and certainly all sexual thoughts are sinful." Most of us are somewhere in that broad middle ground between. From the verse quoted from Matthew 5: 28 it seems clear that at some point in their intensity it is wrong for these fantasies to be directed toward a married person. For the single person, however, it may well provide a partial release of sexual feeling as well as contribute toward a greater acceptance of personal sexuality in general—something which many Christians have tried to repress in a mistaken attitude that sexuality is somehow sinful. Perhaps here, too, there will be a point at which the strength of the fantasy will become too great and an individual may feel wrong in continuing with it. This is again a matter of degree and is up to the individual conscience of the person involved.

Furthermore, it is interesting that in wholesome secular and even religious literature—short stories, novels, and movies—the fantasies of other people are given for our enjoyment, an enjoyment often based on sexual attraction.

Masturbation is another controversy among Christians. In spite of the mythology surrounding the subject, masturbation is not physically destructive nor necessarily psychologically damaging. Yet it often seems to cause a tremendous amount of guilt among Christians, and children are often warned severely against it. In one Christian school a teacher told a group of teenagers they would lose all self-control if they engaged in masturbation. Others have been told they would go insane. I have talked to young people as well as older people who felt that this was the worst sin they had ever committed and that they could have no real relationship with God because of it. One boy I remember was going through real torture over the whole thing.

These attitudes, however, are not unique to Christians alone—at least a few generations back. According to an article in *Human Behavior* magazine, "Some procedures that actually were used for masturbators were clitoridectomy (excision of the clitoris) in girls and women and circumcision and deenervation of the nerves leading to the genital area in boys and men." The article goes on to say that "Nowadays, we tend to regard masturbation as normal . . ." Yet as is true of most things, masturbation can be used to excess. It can be a cop-out for a person who is avoiding some real problems that exist in a marriage, and as such is psychologically damaging for a person who has the availability of a sex partner and yet chooses masturbation instead. For ultimately sex is meant to be an expression of love toward another person. But, depending on why a person masturbates, it can be a constructive way to handle sexual feelings.

Perhaps the major objection one could offer to engaging in either sexual fantasies or masturbation would be the problem of guilt. If either activity engenders guilt, then it becomes harmful unless measures are taken to alleviate that guilt. This is one area where counseling can often be a help.

In addition to the sexual problems which must be handled in a woman's relationship with a man other than her husband, there are other situations which must be dealt with if the relationship is to be healthy. If it is possible to be friends with the wife as well as the husband, that is, of course, ideal. For a woman who is married, the reactions of her own husband to her friendship with another man are important. Some male egos are strong enough to handle such friendships; some are not. No friendship is worth jeopardizing your own marriage. In the same context, the wife of the man with whom you become friendly is important. If she shows signs of unhappiness over the relationship, there again the friendship is not worth hurting the marriage. And again, some wives are more easily threatened and sensitive than others.

Sometimes just small acts of consideration will preserve a friendship without causing jealousy from a mate. When a telephone call is made to a married male friend and his wife answers, talk to her too. Don't act as though she's unimportant. Sometimes the transition from talking to her and then talking to her husband can be made more smoothly by a comment like, "By the way, could I talk to Mark? My committee at church has made some changes that I need some advice on." Or, "I need to talk to John because I haven't been able to catch him at work long enough to say more than two words."

If two couples are at dinner it is unwise of a woman to monopolize the time of the other man to the exclusion of his wife and her own husband. Such behavior is guaranteed to provoke bad feelings. I have seen this happen where the wife who is left out feels that her husband finds her intellectually dull— and she begins to dislike the other woman—and where the husband who is ignored feels defensive and pushed down by his own wife. In general, just normal consideration and good taste will help prevent most problems from arising.

Finally, any woman who has a close relationship with a married man—or a married woman who is close to any man other than her husband—should be careful about her own feelings. Feelings can be controlled—if they aren't fed unwisely by one's fantasy life—and it is easier to behave warmly and yet appropriately if those feelings are not out of control.

In the social involvements which a woman has with men the problems which arise and the rewards which one receives are somewhat different than those which occur in a relationship which is strictly businesslike. Yet increasingly women are being thrown into a daily job where they intermingle and compete with men. In the business world roles become very confused.

A while back a businessman posed a very interesting but frustrating question to me. "What if you had two applicants for an executive job: one male, one female. The woman is the best qualified," he continued, "but the man will do the best job." Confused, I asked him what he meant.

"The woman is without a doubt best," he explained. "However, no one in that office, male *and* female alike, wants a female boss. They won't *let* her do as good a job as the man. Would you hire the person best qualified or the person who would do the best job?" It was a tough, impossible question and one which I suspect is asked repeatedly.

In the business world a woman must be good, really good, to succeed. Unfortunately, in order to push her way ahead, a woman may become overly aggressive in her behavior and declared unfeminine. Some fear this and overcompensate. A woman who is a top specialist in an area of medicine was recently promoted as head of a large research project. As we talked she mentioned resigning from the job, which she really loves, because she "just can't feel right about telling men what to do." If she does quit it will be a waste of talent—and ironically none of the men under her resent her for holding her position because she is so good in the field. She is an unfortunate example of a woman confused over roles in a culture where that confusion starts in childhood—where little boys play doctor and little girls play the nurse who helps the doctor.

On the other hand, some women use their femininity as a weapon with which to gain what they want professionally. Their sexuality is exploited. They are promoted if . . . They get a part in the movie if . . . It is my experience that few women in the business world who are in business for themselves or have executive positions are spared the offer of a better position in trade for a sexual relationship. For some women this is something they accept; for others the price is too high.

In her job a woman will relate to men at various levels—from toleration to perhaps friendship—just as she will relate to women at varying levels from acquaintance to friend. The better the job, however, and the greater the desire to succeed and grow professionally the more she will find the conflict in her role: the conflict between aggressiveness and femininity, the sexual offers, the resentment from even those of her own sex about her leadership.

Yet all is not grim. It's harder to be a woman and

succeed, but many do it and enjoy it. I believe a woman who makes it in the business world, maintains her femininity, and doesn't allow herself to be exploited achieves these ends best by just being herself instead of artificially playing a variety of roles. I once worked under a woman who was the head of the English Department in which I taught. She was organized, well trained and dogmatic in asserting her authority over men and women alike. Yet she was strong enough within herself to let everyone ventilate their opinions in departmental meetings, and if she was proven wrong she would change. She liked feminine clothes, so that was the way she dressed. When any of us were invited to her home we were treated to a lavishly cooked meal served on china and crystal. She was thoroughly comfortable with herself. She wasn't awkwardly playing roles to prove herself. She just was herself and being herself was quite sufficient to gain the respect of those with whom she worked.

Whether as professional colleagues or as social friends—or both—relationships between men and women can be right as well as rewarding. For thirteen years—until his death—C. S. Lewis maintained a friendship through letters with a woman in America whom he never met in person. Through that time he both married and lost to cancer his wife, Joy. He shared these events along with many physical problems and happy times with his American friend. In many ways a private man, Lewis yet felt close enough to this friend to write about intimate feelings, like his fears:

"I'm a panic-y person about money myself

(which is a most shameful confession and a thing dead against Our Lord's words) and poverty frightens me more than anything else except large spiders and the tops of cliffs . . ."

Because his friend had fallen into financial problems, Lewis arranged for her to have a small stipend which has continued on since his death. Friendship? Yes, in the truest sense. Yet one only has to read Lewis' book, *A Grief Observed,* to know the depths of his love and closeness to his own wife.

Friendship is in some ways an elusive thing. For each person that one comes to know, the definition changes and becomes special and unique. Somewhere someone has written words to the effect that "we are molded and shaped by those we love." When that love is directed from a woman toward a man, even in friendship, the responsibility with which the relationship is handled will partially determine what we become. If that relationship is destructive to others, we too will be destroyed. If it is constructive, all involved will be better people for its existence.

Woman at Work

A SMALL BOY MADE A LAST frantic effort to win at the new game we were trying out. It was a game involving both luck and organized thinking. He needed to win and so I hoped that in a final stroke of luck he would. However, I was ahead; so with a last right move I won the game. Angrily Mark looked over at me and exclaimed: "Don't you know, girls aren't supposed to beat boys?"

"Girls aren't supposed to beat boys" is unfortunately the viewpoint of many adults, male and female as well; and children pick up the idea at a very early age. Nor is this concept entirely an outdated male chauvinistic idea, for many women feel exactly the same way. I hear women say things like, "Don't explain the insurance to me; I don't understand things like that. My husband handles those matters," or "I don't understand Bible doctrine. I leave that to my husband. I just try to be a good wife." Yet these same women are offended if someone doubts their intelligence or they become confused if their husband after ten years of marriage turns to another woman because she "can talk to him."

The fact is many men want a woman who is their

intellectual equal. They want to share the responsibilities of marriage and they frequently need a woman with whom they can converse intelligently.

While it is true that there are men who feel threatened by bright women, a bright woman who "plays dumb" to get a man will probably not build a very good marriage. Her intelligence will eventually show and offend her husband or she will play the dumb role throughout a miserable and unchallenging marriage.

In our society there is still a tendency to place a greater value on male intelligence. A girl's education is not always considered as important as a boy's because, after all, a girl will grow up and get married. As a single person, when I converse with married friends very often the male viewpoint predominates. Recently I had dinner with a couple where the man began to voice his strong anti-Semitic views. Extremely outraged, I argued back. His wife just sat there, not agreeing with him but afraid to argue against him. She allowed his opinion to prevail with her while offering the feeble objection of: "Well, dear, are you sure you really feel that way?"

The truth is that women are every bit as intelligent as men, although that intelligence is not always as carefully developed. Marriage should not stop a woman's intellectual development, nor should men be automatically given jobs involving high-powered thinking. A girl of sixteen who, against her inclination, plans a secretarial future from the time she begins high school because that's what's expected of her should reconsider. If she prefers to become a physician and has that kind of ability, why should she become anything else? On the other hand, if a young boy is expected to be educated toward joining his father's law firm but prefers interior decorating and has real talent for that, why shouldn't he do what he is best suited for? Why should women be file clerks and waitresses while men study for law, medicine or engineering? To go further, what's wrong with a woman as a plumber if it's what she wants to be? She'll make a lot more money than most women's jobs pay. And don't argue that being a plumber is not ladylike or is too degrading! Not unless you remove all the underpaid women who clean toilets in public institutions or those that clean up at convalescent homes and hospitals.

Yet as firmly as I believe in women and men both being freed to do a job for which they have talent and interest, I do not feel good about these jobs being given or taken as mere tokens. Once it became obvious that women could handle a television news show as well as a man, within a short period of time one woman appeared on each evening news presentation. Never three women and no men, or two women and one man, or just three good men. It is hard for me to believe that of all the people interested in that kind of job one woman was always better than other male applicants or that at times a second woman might not have been better than a male newscaster who got the job.

The same principle has been true in the civil rights movement. Blacks at first appeared, one by one. One in a food commercial, one on a documentary, one in a given factory or school. Races that didn't complain, like the Orientals or the American Indians, were rarely seen at all. They didn't require a token to silence them.

Tokens are a necessary start, I suppose, but they bother me. It would be nice to feel that race and sex didn't matter in getting a job. In a country like ours where competition has always been so important it would be admirable if people went into a vocation and got jobs because they were good and well-trained, not because they were women, or not women.

For many Christians, however, the question is not so much a matter of whether or not a woman is as intelligent as a man, but again of the appropriateness of her role. Is it appropriate for a Christian woman to use her intellectual capacities to their fullest? Three women, one in the Old Testament and two in the New Testament, provide a key to answering that question.

Deborah became a leader in Israel at the time that King Jabin of Canaan was making life unbearable for Israel. In Judges 4: 3 (TLB) we read that he had "made life unbearable for the Israelis for twenty years."

Deborah was the wife of Lappidoth. Apparently during that time she was also a person to whom many people came for counsel. At the peak of the problem with Jabin, Deborah called a top military leader, Barak, and told him of the need to defeat Jabin's army and his General, Sisera.

After they drew up plans, Barak agreed to go after Jabin, but with one stipulation: "I'll go, but only if you go with me."

Deborah agreed, but with a counter warning: "I'll go with you; but I'm warning you now that the honor of conquering Sisera will go to a woman instead of to you!"

Their efforts were successful. Deborah's military orders proved effective and "after that there was peace in the land for forty years."

While Deborah was a politician and military leader, another woman, Lydia, who lived after the time of Christ, was a businesswoman. Acts 16: 14 (TLB) describes her as a "saleswoman from Thyatira, a merchant of purple cloth." Whether or not she was married is not stated in the Bible but it seems clear that her business was both successful and her own.

After her conversion to Christianity, her acceptance by such church leaders as Paul and Silas is made obvious by the fact that they came and stayed at her home. It is probable that her home became somewhat of a haven for them since they returned there again later after their release from jail.

Different from both Deborah and Lydia was Priscilla. Priscilla was a Jewish woman who left Rome with her husband Aquila as a result of Jewish persecution. They finally ended up in Ephesus where both of them earned a living as tent-makers.

Both Priscilla and her husband were very involved in the New Testament church and apparently they were well taught in New Testament doctrine. For when Apollos came to speak at Ephesus, they recognized his lack of New Testament knowledge and "afterwards they met with him and explained what had happened to Jesus since the time of John, and all that it meant" (Acts 18: 26, TLB). Yet Apollos himself was already considered a remarkable Bible teacher.

That Priscilla herself was considered a woman who was intelligent and powerful in the early church is further proven by historical facts other than those recorded in the Bible. According to *All of the Women of the Bible* by Edith Deen: "Tertullian records, 'By the holy Prisca, the gospel is preached.' One of the oldest catacombs of Rome—the Coemeterium Priscilla, was named in her honor. And a church, 'Titulus St. Prisca,' was erected on the Aventine in Rome. It bore the inscription 'Titulus Aquila et Prisca.' Prisca's name appears often on monuments of Rome. And 'Acts of St. Prisca' was a legendary writing popular in the tenth century."

A politician and military leader—Deborah; a successful businesswoman who owned her own home—Lydia; and a church leader—Priscilla: All three gave every evidence of superior intellect. All three had great qualities of leadership. Yet all three kept their own homes, were better than average as hostesses in those homes, and two at least were married. Their lives seem to reinforce the idea that women are capable of performing superior intellectual tasks, and furthermore that from a Scriptural point of view such performance is spiritually appropriate and is not an indication of masculinity in a woman.

It is safe to assume that God does not ordinarily waste talent which He has given. In both men and women there are varying degrees of intellectual ability and other talents, such as ability in art. If a woman finds she has both the ability and the inclination to contribute something to society she should not be held back because she is a woman. Nor should a man be pushed ahead into an area for which he is not suited just because he is a man.

In a church I once attended a young man was urged to become Sunday School Superintendent because "he was such a good Christian." He completely lacked creativity and was not particularly sensitive to the needs of children. To make sure he didn't completely fail, his wife carefully planned each Sunday's program with him and he faithfully followed her instructions. When a special program was approaching, she would again plan the format for him. He never learned how to do it on his own, but I was always amused when I heard someone compliment him for an idea that was never his in the first place.

The sad part lay in the effect it had on the marriage. Instead of doing something he could do well, the husband felt inadequate functioning as a puppet. Yet he knew that to play such a role was his only way of survival in the job. His wife, on the other hand, felt a little angry at having to hide her ability and frustrated because she knew the effect the whole situation was having on her husband.

It is unrealistic to assume that men are always brighter than women. It is plain stupid to know that and yet play the role of the intellectually deficient wife or the all-knowing male. Women are not always beneath men in intelligence. Yet I have seen men go through agony trying to promote a superior image, hoping their fallibility would not be discovered. And as a woman I have felt the frustration of playing down something I genuinely knew because I was afraid it would threaten a male ego. I have learned long since that when men and women who have a good relationship interact in a more relaxed way, both will exhibit their strong and weak points to varying degrees and yet neither will usually feel threatened by the other. To roleplay only makes a relationship shallow and unnatural or at times it only prolongs an unrewarding friendship between people who probably are so incompatible they wouldn't be friends if they really let down with each other.

There is, however, a real practical problem involved when a woman uses her abilities, particularly if she is married and increasingly so if she has children. A woman who has a job or writes or does crafts or runs for a political office will often find these things running in conflict with her role as a wife and mother. The answer does not altogether lie in adding these activities to her life; there must frequently be an alteration of her life-style.

Whether it comes by better organization or extra help from a maid or gardener, a woman needs to be careful that in developing some of her abilities she doesn't just add to an overburdened schedule. One woman already maintains a large house and garden; takes her son to Little League twice a week, Boy Scouts once a week, and the YMCA on Saturdays; takes her daughter to the Brownies once a week, piano lessons once a week, and makes frequent trips to the orthodontist. Add to these grocery shopping, errands to the shoe repair and post office, and countless impromptu trips here and there and you have a schedule that's already too full. Car pools for the children and warning the family that trips to places like the shoe repair or cleaners will only be made at a certain time each week will help preserve precious time that can better be used elsewhere.

The woman who works full time will need the cooperation of her children and husband in doing household tasks. One woman I know is urged to work full time by her husband because they need the money, and yet he really balks at any suggestion that he help with the housework. In contrast, a woman who spends a great deal of time in artistic endeavors does them late at night when the children are in bed. In order to let her sleep later in the morning, her husband regularly gets up and makes breakfast. Since she is home in the afternoon and uses that time to be with her children, she makes sure that each evening she has an inviting dinner for her husband, at the time of day when he is most tired and appreciates the attention. In this way they each support each other's endeavors and show a mutual consideration which has deepened their love for each other. The wife is not deprived of her own pursuits and as a result she is a happier person and a better marriage partner.

Every woman should pursue the interests and talents God has given her. Whether it be by a method as undramatic as reading a book each afternoon or as dramatic as an outside job it will tend to raise her feelings of worth and thus better her relationships with others, including her family.

For women who have to work to support themselves but don't enjoy that work, or for women who feel like they are dissatisfied with household tasks consuming all their lives, the pursuit of something else which interests them will add greater meaning to their lives. I have known women to work part time with handicapped children, teach a Bible study, do various types of art work, write magazine articles, work for political campaigns and engage in any number of other activities which have greatly enhanced their lives.

For some women the answer to their intellectual fulfillment will be in a full-time commitment to a career. Others may combine a career with a marriage.

Still others may find most of their fulfillment to be within the home, and yet they will wisely develop other interests which will keep them from stagnating. Each should find that fulfillment in her own way. But she should not be limited by the notion that as a woman she is not intellectually suited for competition with men.

A woman is as capable of intellectual pursuits as a man. And for the Christian woman there is every Biblical evidence that God does not expect her to hide that ability. The degree to which she develops that ability and the vehicle she uses are up to her.

Woman As Divorcée

A WOMAN IN HER MID-THIRTIES sat across from me with an agonizing question: whether or not it was right for her to get a divorce. Jan and her husband were both Christians, but following his time in Vietnam, Rick had changed. He was critical of his wife and at times seemed dangerously irrational. The night before Jan saw me he had picked up a knife in anger over a trivial incident, and chased his four-year-old son waving the knife and shouting threats.

Psychologically he was destructive to his family. He would look at his six-year-old daughter, Jennifer, and say things like, "You're ugly," or "How come you can't be more like other kids your age?" Jan too came in for her share of his verbal abuse which was greatly affecting her feelings of self-esteem. But what concerned her most was her fear of the effect he was having on her two small children during their formative years when children develop their basic self-image. Already after a year of this the children were having nightmares and becoming abnormally shy and were afraid of people. Then too she feared what he might someday do in a real act of violence.

Jan had tried everything, from applying spiritual principles to her marriage to psychological counseling. Rick refused any offers of help. Now, after the knife incident could she really stay with him any longer? Did she have the right to get a divorce?

Everyone she had talked to at her church had a different viewpoint ranging from, "Stay with him and leave it in God's hands," to "Since there is no sexual immorality involved, you don't have a Scriptural basis for divorce; but this must be an exception somehow. You obviously can't live with him." Somehow none of these viewpoints appeared to be completely satisfactory. She seemed to be in a dilemma which gave her no right way out.

It is relatively easy to talk about a woman's role in handling a divorce emotionally and in helping her children to adjust. It is far harder to deal with a woman's role in the rightness or wrongness of that divorce. Yet that very point seems to be the place where this discussion should begin.

Matthew 5: 32 is the most concise statement on divorce given by Christ in the Gospels. "I tell you that every man who puts away his wife except on the ground of unfaithfulness causes her to commit adultery, and whoever marries her when so divorced commits adultery" (Weymouth).

"Unfaithfulness" here is translated "fornication" in the King James Version and means a sexual act which is immoral. This could include an act of incest, adultery, child molestation, homosexuality, sadism, etc. It seems apparent that the word implies an actual act and that the meaning goes beyond that of only adultery.

However, the real question that Christ is answering in Matthew is whether a man should be able to divorce a woman "for every cause." According to the Jewish law of the time a man could get a divorce for almost any reason. When the question was asked of Christ, "Is it lawful for a man to put away his wife for every cause?" (Mt. 19: 3), the Pharisees were probably trying to trap Christ. It was not an honest question from those seeking after truth.

Even the Rabbis, representing the religious establishment, disagreed on their opinion as to the grounds of divorce. One school of interpretation allowed divorce for such a trivial act as a burned supper. Contrary to the Jewish ideal, marriage was often a mockery. In one case recorded by Alfred Edersheim, two rabbis decided to each marry a woman for a day and then divorce her.

Women were the real victims of the looseness of the Jewish laws. Because a woman under Jewish law could not divorce a man and because the culture did not provide much opportunity for women who wished to support themselves, women were in danger of being thrown out on the street and left in a pretty helpless position if their husbands divorced them.

In the Greek and Roman cultures of the first century A.D., women were allowed a divorce legally. Economically, however, a woman would have a hard time supporting herself without a husband. Perhaps this is one reason for the high incidence of prostitution at that time. So in these cultures too a woman could be caused great suffering by a divorce.

While human suffering was not Christ's primary motive, the result of Christ's rather strict pronouncement on divorce had the effect of protecting women from the harshness of divorce in these cultures. Less suffering would seem to come this way than under the older, more permissive structure.

But the problem of Jan and her husband still remains, for with them there had been no immoral sexual act. I have heard some pastors use I Corinthians 7: 10, 11 to resolve such a problem: "And unto the married I command, yet not I, but the Lord, let not the wife depart from her husband: but and if she depart, let her remain unmarried, or be reconciled to her husband: and let not the husband put away his wife."

The motive for such use of these verses is perhaps understandable but is not according to good Biblical interpretation. Paul clearly says, "Let not the wife depart from the husband." While these verses may represent a softening position, they do not really justify even a legal separation, much less a divorce.

We are dealing with a gray area. In one of his books, Viktor Frankl describes his emotions as he and his wife face internment by the Nazis—and possible death. He asks his wife to make him one promise, that if she is confronted with the choice of having sex with someone else or execution that she will choose to submit herself sexually. For, reasons Frankl, to choose death for oneself is a greater wrong than adultery. The only possible choice in such a situation is to choose the lesser of the two evils.

From one point of view Jan's dilemma is similar. She is wrong in allowing herself and her children to be destroyed and yet she, according to many, is wrong if she leaves him. In such a situation a decision might be made in terms of what seems most right, or, to pick up Walter Trobisch's idea, what is most loving.

Along somewhat different lines, if we take the Bible as a book of principles and then view the Scriptural stance on divorce within its cultural context we arrive at a perspective which some may find helpful. So, for example, when Paul commands a woman to have her head covered in the local church the basic principle is that of appearing moral. Prostitutes went out with their heads uncovered, not women with morals. Therefore the principle is to both be and appear moral. The application of the principle for that day was to wear a head covering. Yet apart from the Catholic church and such groups as the Plymouth Brethren, most Christians today agree that women can go to church without hats.

The principle which Christ states in connection with divorce is that of the sanctity of marriage. The oneness which is epitomized in the sexual union is the image used in connection with Christ and the Church. This principle was applied to the Jewish-Greek-Roman world as giving grounds for divorce on the basis of sexual immorality only.

Yet in a culture like ours where women are fully able to support themselves and where there are social and legal institutions to protect women and children, it is perhaps possible to make a different application as long as one adheres to Christ's principle of the sanctity of marriage. Perhaps in such a setting a divorce or a legal separation—I don't pretend to know which—might be the right move for a Christian who finds his or her marriage remaining deeply and permanently destructive, even after much time, effort, and professional counseling have been put into making the marriage work. Such a relationship would seem to destroy the meaning of any sexual union as completely as sexual immorality. Indeed hate and destructiveness would seem to make such union a mockery. I once heard a young woman say that once two people had sex they were married in God's sight. I have wondered since if she would feel the same way about rape. The sex act is not always a sacred one—but it is certainly *meant* to be sacred.

The answers in this area are not always clear as is evidenced by the number of scholars who disagree. And certainly one must be exceedingly careful in interpreting the Bible according to a changing cultural setting, especially on a subject which the Bible speaks about as seriously as it does on divorce and adultery (the latter was punishable by death in the Old Testament). Yet in James 1 we are promised wisdom if we ask in faith, and each of us ultimately must take that wisdom in application to our own consciences.*

We have looked at the role women played historically in the matter of divorce and how that role would affect the grounds for divorce or legal separation in our own age. But equally important to the role women play in the grounds for a divorce is the role they play when that divorce actually takes place.

Following a divorce the various roles that a woman plays may change drastically, probably more for her than for the man. While loneliness is probably acutely felt by both, it may be felt more deeply by the woman who has been in a more dependent role. Sleeping alone and eating alone, waking up in the middle of the night to find no one there; these all can be deeply painful to a woman who has never really been alone before. As one woman put it: "I used to wake up and reach out to touch him and he wasn't there."

When guilt and rejection are felt in the middle of loneliness, the problem becomes even greater. There is often guilt over whether more could have been done to save the marriage. Feelings of rejection, too, gnaw away at many as they feel that if somehow they had been a better person this wouldn't have happened. Women wonder if they've lost their attractiveness, or if the "other woman" was more interesting.

Counseling is often a help to women involved in a divorce, and it should not be shunned as though it implied failure or lack of trust in God. But apart from or in addition to counseling, very simple, practical things may help.

One woman going through a divorce found herself first staying at home, and then in bed. She simply wanted to withdraw. Such a simple task as going to the grocery store was agony, but she *had* to make that effort if she wanted to pull out of her depression. She did, and along with the help of counseling she became a whole person again. Another woman developed some talent in art, a talent which had lain dormant for years but now became an absorbing hobby. Another woman began going to a weekly women's Bible study where she was not only helped spiritually but where she found some very good friends. Other women become volunteers at a hospital or work part time.

But for most women who get a divorce or legal separation the biggest role change is that they must go out and get a job in order to support themselves.

While these women need to also develop their social lives, a bulk of their time will be taken up in work. For an untrained woman in particular, this is difficult. She may find herself in a low-paying, boring job. Unfortunately, along with this she may find even such tasks as keeping a checking account and calling a plumber new and difficult. One woman found calling a doctor for her sick child an almost traumatic experience. "Do I dare call him without first calling my husband?" she asked me.

For a woman who finds herself in this spot, additional job training may help and perhaps the advice of friends may provide answers for some of the practical problems that arise in a home. The real answer, however, lies in preparation beforehand. It is wise for a woman to be trained in some skill. And no husband should shelter his wife so that she can't handle the money and be informed on such problems as house payments and insurance. Certainly one does not anticipate divorce, but these same problems are faced by widows too. And in the emotional upheaval of a divorce or death a woman is more comfortable if she can already drive, handle the business of the home, and if necessary go out and get a job.

Another role that changes is her role with the children. If a woman has to work she will spend less time with her children and may feel guilty about that. Because of her guilt she may spend more money on them "to make up for it," or she may avoid any social life for herself. Both are destructive. Actually it is the quality of the time that is spent with children that counts, not the quantity. A woman who works has a life of her own socially and then spends time with her children which she and they enjoy, is more

86

effective than the guilt-ridden mother who spends lots of time with them but resents every minute of it.

In many other ways a woman's role changes during a divorce, uniquely for each person. Yet perhaps for the Christian woman one of the hardest changes to handle is the feeling that you are alone with your friends who are married and in a church where some look down on you for being divorced. The stigma is still there. In some places a woman is even restricted as to her participation in church activities—such as taking part in the communion service. It is here that the church has a responsibility to treat this person who has already suffered so much in a way that really shows deep Christian love.

Amy Carmichael hits at the core of this when she says in *Gold by Moonlight*:

God forgive us for the strange coldness of so much of our love. The calculating love of Christians is the shame of the church and the astonishment of angels. By Thine agony and bloody sweat; by Thy cross and passion; by Thy precious death and burial; by the glorious resurrection and ascension; and by the coming of the Holy Ghost, from the sin of coldness, Good Lord, deliver us.

*For those who wish to pursue the matter more fully, I recommend reading such books as *Divorce* by John R. W. Stott; *Divorce and Remarriage* by Guy Duty; *My Wife Made Me a Polygamist* and *I Married You*, both by Walter Trobisch.

Woman in Church

A WOMAN IS ORDAINED as a minister in one church. In a church a few blocks away she is not allowed to speak or even pray in a church meeting where men are present. Yet if she is a well known missionary and sends tapes home, those tapes will be played to men and women alike. If she has a good voice (or even one not so good), she can sing a solo at any church meeting. At another church a woman can hold no office of leadership but she can paint her Sunday school room and act as taxi driver for visiting ministers.

Even in churches where women are allowed to use their intellectual gifts, innuendos and remarks sometimes cut through and minimize those efforts. The husband of a talented Bible teacher quipped kiddingly to a male friend that his wife was "due for another beating." His friend laughed and repeated the story.

If women in the world in general feel frustrated and confused by the conflict in their roles, so does that same conflict appear as great or greater within the church. Many women avoid the conflict altogether and just slip into the social butterfly role with women's luncheons and teas or into a work with children or women where no one can question their role. Yet at home they are often the controlling force behind their husbands. They have their voice, but subtly—almost deceptively.

The Biblical view of a woman's role in the church is reasonably forward looking and progressive, particularly in light of the restrictions on women in the culture of that time. In fact the view of women held in the early church was often more progressive than that of many churches today. It is true that I Timothy 2:12 (The Living Bible) says, "I never let women teach men or lord it over them. Let them be silent in your church meetings." Yet in I Corinthians 11:16 (TLB) Paul says, "A woman should wear a covering when prophesying or praying publicly in the church. . . ." Contradictory? No! But certainly in need of clarification within the context of the text and the culture.

Since prophesying is the greatest gift included in the Corinthians' list, and includes preaching or teaching, and since prophesying is granted to women publicly in the church, the I Corinthians passage seems in conflict with the passage in I Timothy. Yet if once again we remember that the Bible is a book of principles it makes the interpretation of these verses easier.

To me it is impossible to escape the principle of male authority in New Testament church order, as in marriage. In I Corinthians 11:10 Paul talks of the woman's head covering as a "sign that she is under man's authority." Yet he hastens to say in verses 11 and 12 that before God both are the same. In the two passages we have been dealing with, Paul seems to be talking against a woman as the chief authority in a church, but from the verses in I Corinthians he does not seem to be forbidding other types of female leadership and teaching. Thus there is a problem with a woman in the top position of church leadership, but not in her having a teaching ministry or other positions of leadership in the local church.

Cultural influences too cannot be ignored, for the passages are full of obvious cultural references. Women wore head coverings as a sign of morality in those days since prostitutes went about with their heads uncovered, a fact which is no longer true in our culture. A hat today represents vanity, if anything, certainly not modesty. Paul's statement that it is natural for men to have short hair is also very cultural since in many early cultures men wore long hair almost exclusively.

However, the important point for our consideration is the fact that from a Biblical standpoint women have an intellectual function in the church. They were not meant to be restricted exclusively to the nursery, the choir, the Sunday school (for children) and the kitchen, although for many these are places of valuable service.

Many of the prominent women in the New Testament church beautifully blended an intellectual role with the more traditionally feminine one. As has been mentioned, Priscilla was one of the main leaders of the early church. She had a vital teaching ministry while at the same time she provided a haven in her home for church leaders like Paul.

Another woman, Phebe, was described by Paul in Romans 16 as a "servant of the church" and "a succourer of many. . . ." It is thought that she probably was entrusted with the delivery of the epistle to the Romans, since at that time such a letter to Rome had to be carried by a private messenger.

The word "servant" comes from the Greek word "deacon" which has led some to infer that she was a deaconess. Dr. Anna Starr in *The Bible Status of Woman* feels that Phebe was a minister like the apostle Paul.

At any rate, she was a church leader and highly respected. Yet she was, like Priscilla, a person who often entertained Christians; and it appears that she at one time nursed Paul through a long illness. As a parenthesis, her long trip to Rome would probably be considered quite improper by the standards of *Fascinating Womanhood* where women are told not to travel long distances alone!

Dorcas was a New Testament woman who was more domestic than some. Dorcas was known for her "good works and almsdeeds" (Acts 9: 36). She lived at a seaport, Joppa, and apparently had money. From the description of her we must conclude that she did many helpful things for people which went beyond the giving of money.

Thus the Biblical view of a woman's role is a balanced one. She is portrayed as an intelligent, capable, hospitable being with varying gifts. And it is this variety which we need to accept.

Furthermore the fact that a woman's role in the church is in some ways different from that of a man does not mean that she has less value. In a competitive society like ours, leadership is often felt to be a mark of superiority. Yet before God other services have tremendous value. Thus Christ, who without debate would be considered to have inestimable worth, washed the feet of his disciples and with his own hands fed the hungry multitudes who had gathered to hear Him speak.

Along the same lines Christ said to His disciples as they squabbled over their status in Christ's Kingdom:

"Whoever wishes to be great among you must be your servant, and whoever desires to be first among you must be your slave; just as the Son of man came not to be waited on but to serve . . ." (Mt. 20: 26-28, Amplified).

Then, after uttering those words, Christ left Jericho and met two blind men who pleaded with Him to heal them. "And Jesus in pity touched their eyes . . . "thus demonstrating His role as a Helper of men, a Servant.

Perhaps God's view of the importance of a woman's role in the church is clarified by looking at His view of the importance of practical acts of service. And such a view further explains why Paul could be consistent in presenting a woman's role as including acceptance, ultimately, of male authority in the church, and yet at the same time he could stress that before God there is neither male nor female. The *position* is secondary but the *value* is not.

Viewed in this light, a woman's role in the church is not one of constantly trying to fight for her rights but rather of expanding the tremendous ministry she has—which again does include teaching and some forms of leadership. Yet very often the service of helping others is not so showy. I know one woman who helped a drug addict for months until this person began to gradually see that perhaps she did have some worth and that God really did love her. It took long phone calls, often at night, tons of patience, many lunches together and much wisdom. Only God will know the real effort that went into rebuilding this person—and only eternity will show the greatness of the reward.

One woman I know has a gift and desire for prayer. Praying has been for years her chief function in the church. Another woman is one of the best Bible teachers I have known, but she rather dislikes housework. Another has her house open constantly for visitors who need a meal or a place to stay. One woman is helpful with the sick and is faithful in her visitation; another has endless patience with children. Still another is a brilliant organizer of church materials and programs. Another is a musician. Many combine several of these qualities.

In both male and female roles within the church there is great variety. While the Bible seems to teach that men are to have the ultimate authority, women and men alike will fill positions of leadership. And while women seem peculiarly suited to helping others, women and men alike will also fit into this role. Here again, the woman's role, like that of a man, includes a variety of services.

Women, like men, cannot be stereotyped. They have a variety of interests and talents and each person's role in the church should fit with his or her unique potential.

There are, however, certain women who have particular problems within a church. One such group of women are those who are relatively young but unmarried. This group includes women who have never been married, those who are widowed at an early age and those who are divorced. Isolation is a primary difficulty, for in the small, local church there are very few men or women between the ages of twenty-five and sixty who are unmarried. In larger churches there are more, but they are frequently grouped together apart from the rest of the church.

A while back I visited a singles group in a moderately large church. A friend who was divorced went with me. As we walked in she looked around and then turned to me and said: "Let's go. Do we really have to do this?" Somehow that feeling of reticence which we both experienced expressed a reaction—not against individuals in that group, but against the total atmosphere. Some people in that group could have provided meaningful relationships for each other, and perhaps some of them did. But there was a prevailing atmosphere which focused exclusively on finding a mate. It was inherent in the jokes, in the side glances, in the questions asked. The result was a self-occupation which militated against the formation of any broader relationship.

Other experiences in singles groups have been equally dismal. Yet I'm sure that somewhere there are some groups in which more meaningful relationships develop. However, from what I have experienced, and from what my patients and friends have encountered, many single men and women in many churches simply throw themselves into a teaching job or work in the choir and make friends that way. They are then in contact with married people and other single people who don't feel like stagnating in an isolated group.

Yet group contact is important and for that reason I am glad to see that many large churches are now arranging groups by topic studied, not by marital status. If this trend progresses it will solve some of the social and even spiritual problems of single people who feel isolated or left out in the church program.

There is mutual benefit in church groups mixing both single and married persons. A single woman or man has a different life-style and perhaps a greater variety of experiences than a married person. Likewise, a married person has her own background and interests which contribute to her relationship with other people.

Married women often admit to me their need for the stimulation of conversation which revolves around something other than babies and new detergents. Single women also need a perspective other than that offered in the business world. Furthermore, single women need to relate to people as people, not as potential mates in a church marriage mill.

And increasingly, many younger people are choosing not to get married, not because they can't, but for a lot of reasons which are valid for them. For one thing, the stigma against not being married is a lot less than it used to be, and so people are not so prone to marry just anybody in order to be socially acceptable.

Thus, the single woman in the church must not only fit into a role as a woman who contributes to and receives benefit from church relationships, but she must overcome the isolation of singleness if she is to have a role at all. It is the spiritual obligation of the church to help her do this by providing acceptance as well as meaningful social activities and opportunities for service. In the long run the church will benefit, for single people often have more time and money to contribute to a church than if they were married.

Another large group of women who often find they have little role at all in the church except to be there, is the large number of widows of retirement age. Their problems and potential are both great, and the Scriptures give detailed instructions regarding them.

In I Timothy 5: 3 (TLB) Paul writes: "The church should take loving care of women whose husbands have died, if they don't have anyone else to help them. But if they have children or grandchildren, these are the ones who should take the responsibility, for kindness should begin at home, supporting needy parents. This is something that pleases God very much." There is another qualification for a widow's receiving help from the church, besides the absence of relatives. According to verse five, they must be "looking to God for his help and spending much time in prayer . . . not . . . spending their time running around gossiping, seeking only pleasure. . . ."

Regarding those people who won't support their own relatives, Paul says they have no right to call themselves Christians.

Thus the admonition in this matter is strong—to the church, to the family *and* to the widow herself. Every provision is made for her sustenance so that she can continue to function as a worthwhile human being. And besides the humanitarian aspects of Biblical teaching, clearly there is the idea that the widow will be a contributing being. In Titus 2: 3-5 (TLB),

"The older women [are] to be quiet and respect-
ful in everything they do. They must not go
around speaking evil of others and must not be
heavy drinkers, but they should be teachers of
goodness. These older women must train the
younger women to live quietly, to love their
husbands and their children, and to be sensible
and clean minded, spending their time in their
own homes, being kind and obedient to their
husbands, so that the Christian faith can't be
spoken against by those who know them."

In I Timothy 5: 9 a special office is set up for
certain older widows of at least sixty years of age.
The qualifications are: one marriage; a good reputa-
tion for having done good; well brought up children;
kindness to strangers as well as to Christians; kindness to the sick and hurt; and a constant readiness
to show kindness.

In essence a woman who has successfully fulfilled
her role as a woman is then qualified to instruct
others in a special way. All widows are encouraged
to function in this way to a degree. But those who
qualify are given a very special function.

This widow's list to which Paul refers is a little
vague in meaning and has been a matter of debate
among theologians. According to Conybeare it could
refer to those supported from the general fund, or to
a list of deaconesses, or to church-widows referred
to by Tertullian as having distinct ecclesiastical position and duties—female presbyters. I tend to support
the third viewpoint since age sixty is a little old to
be called as a deaconess and since other widows
than this select group were certainly supported by
the church.

Widowhood is thus presented as a time of great potential in service, not as the end of a life, the start of old age, the time to deteriorate and complain and hope for death.

The concept of effective service in old age is something we Americans have trouble accepting, for we fight age with cosmetics, face lifts, health spas and out-and-out denial. We glorify youth and try to deny the existence of death itself by ignoring it until it hits us. Even then we camouflage its reality with our elaborate and expensive burial rites.

I once had the privilege of living with a Chinese family where the attitudes of their culture were far different. Death was not embraced, but it was accepted as a normal function of life. Age was revered and looked forward to. When a grandmother of the house reached seventy she was given the biggest celebration of anyone in the house—and the best gift! Sixteen was unimportant compared to seventy! To reach seventy was an achievement and deserved recognition. A woman of seventy had really the most important role of her life in that now people respected her and listened to her.

The argument might be raised that many older widows do not seem to have the "wisdom of age," that they aren't people who fulfill a role of respect. Perhaps there are two reasons: their own neglect in building toward this role and assuming it, for in a sense we are in youth and middle age what we shall become as we get older; and our society's emphasis on the uselessness of age. And, deny it or not, we do have that attitude. An attitude which is not only psychologically destructive but spiritually unsound. If you tell a person they are useless and "over the hill" long enough, they begin to believe you and act accordingly. Society itself will not make the needed changes so the new attitude will have to come through the church.

Referring to the Church as the Body of Christ, Paul says: "The eye can never say to the hand, 'I don't need you.' The head can't say to the feet, 'I don't need you.'" Nor can the church say to the widow, "I don't need you."

Married or single, old or young, women have a vital role in the church. They are not just the window dressing. They are a vital, substantial part of the whole. The role of the individual woman, while it may have guidelines, is fluid enough to be fulfilled uniquely in each woman. And as a woman assumes her role she and the church will be more whole as a result.

Woman As Individual

A NINE-YEAR-OLD WHO I SAW in counseling sessions for a number of months happily announced to me that she had finally decided that she was smart and that she wanted to become a doctor. Another little girl about two years younger has become committed to the idea of writing books. They are both bright children and even at these ages seem somewhat suited for these professions. Joanne, the first child, has a love for math and a competitive determination that may well lead her into the medical field. Laura, the second, is perceptive and sensitive and very verbal when she is comfortable with a person. It has not entered either of their heads that being a woman could be a drawback or that "it's a man's world out there." Rather, they are growing up in families and in a culture where women are uniquely free to develop their vocational interests.

It is true, there is still inequality between men and women—but not as much as there used to be. Little girls are not as apt to grow up thinking they have to be nurses because they can't become doctors. If they want to be nurses, it's more often because that's what they really want to be. Culturally, we still have conflicting roles, but at least that is better than one repressive position which all women are supposed to fit into. And when one works from the viewpoint of Christianity the role of a woman becomes more focused and less confusing. Thus the Christian woman in American society has the clarity of purpose set forth in the Bible—which allows great development of ability—and the advantages of a society which is daily opening doors for women. With these advantages, however, comes unique responsibility. Women can no longer hide behind discrimination as a copout for not doing anything, because discrimination, while it exists, is not generally strong enough to be prohibitive. Nor can a woman claim that as a Christian she should withdraw from any intellectual challenge because clearly that is not what the Scriptures say. A woman is thus confronted with the choice of becoming what she wants to be—of being uniquely a woman in the way she wishes to fulfill that role.

Alice is a woman in her late thirties. She is married, has three children and has never worked in a job outside of her home. If she had never married she would have probably been a commercial artist since she went to art school and was developing those talents when she met Ken. She still paints, exhibits and even sells paintings. But her first love is her home and family.

Her home is warm and artistic and she is a source of refuge and help to many people who stop by for lunch or afternoon coffee. Every Saturday morning she bakes bread and makes some homemade cookies —from scratch! Her lampshades are products of a class she took at the local high school, as are an occasional hooked rug or upholstered chair.

Her children are always put to bed with a story. On rainy days they know that the evening meal will be special and that there will usually be a fire in the fireplace. They've grown used to homebaked food and handmade doll clothes.

Alice has chosen a life-style which suits her and pleases her family. It's right for *her*.

Nicolle, on the other hand, has chosen a very different way of life. She too is married, but she is also the editor of a thriving Christian magazine. She is deeply involved in her work and in issues that arise from it, like women's rights. Her viewpoints are balanced and far from fanatical but she is without doubt a person committed to writing and editing in a way that will have a spiritual impact on people's lives and change them. Nicolle and Alice are both dedicated Christians but their life commitments are different. Nicolle couldn't care less if her house were filled with needlepoint done with her hands, while Alice is largely indifferent to the idea of making an impact on the world which exists outside of her own family and friends.

Nicolle loves to cook and she keeps a home that is attractive and comfortable. But when it's a choice between home-baked bread or a good article for her magazine, the article wins out. Michael, her husband, is different, too, from Ken. Mike likes a wife who is involved outside of the home and finds that her interests make for interesting conversation. He understands, too, that with her outside work she is unable to always keep up with the work at home, and so he often suggests dinner out in order to lessen the strain on Nicolle. Nicolle's mother is of the old school of thought; she would like Nicolle to settle down and raise six children. But in all honesty to herself, Nicolle can't just walk away from a way of life that is important to her—and to *add* six children to her already busy life would be unfair to them, to her, and to her marriage with Mike. Someday, perhaps they will have a child, or adopt one. But right now that is not at the top of her priorities.

Claire, on the other hand, is different still from Alice and Nicolle. Claire is also in her thirties, unmarried, and a research scientist with a doctoral degree in Bacteriology. Once a few years back she was deeply in love with a heart surgeon. But, maybe because both of them were so absorbed in their work, the romance ended.

While at times Claire wishes she had a husband, she values her freedom too. Her research often sends her to foreign countries where she works for several months on a project or on lecture tours within the United States.

Her personal life is far from dull. She dates and she has a variety of female friends as well, including some who are married. As a Christian woman in the field of science she has made valuable contributions in working with student groups on several university campuses. Claire has desires for a home and children, for a husband, for sex—but she has put such a high priority on her professional life that only a very unique marital arrangement could fit with her lifestyle. But once again, for *her* this is the life-style she has chosen.

Alice, Nicolle and Claire fill very different roles. And, of course, there are countless women who fit in between these three roles. But the important point is that they have each chosen to shape their lives uniquely. All are distinctly feminine; all wish they had time to be all three types of women. Claire would like to sew. Alice would like to travel more. Nicolle would like to have more time at home than she does. Both Claire and Nicolle think they may want children someday, and sometimes Alice wishes she didn't have any! But all three have been smart enough to know that they can't do everything, and especially not all at once.

One of the greatest dangers in the fact that women in our society have been given greater choices and opportunities is that society has still tended to dictate a certain rigid ideal of femininity. A woman must marry, raise children, make homemade Christmas gifts, cook gourmet dinners—and then she can be an editor, writer, scientist, social reformer or anything else she feels directed toward. *No* woman can do that. A few may *look* like they can. But look deeply into their lives and you'll find out that it doesn't happen that way.

With the gift of choice comes the necessity of priorities. What do you want to do with your life as a woman? What talents and direction are you sensing as you lay this matter before God? Then do it and don't feel guilty about what you can't do. A well-known missionary once said to me: "Don't ever let anyone make you feel guilty because you're not superactive in the local church. What you are doing outside of the church is more valuable, in your case, than anything you could do within. *And you can't do both.*" He recognized *me* as an individual. The advice was for *my* life commitment, not for someone else.

Femininity is a much deeper thing than baking a

cake or dusting a chair. It's an aura that one has. It shows in the way one speaks and looks and responds to people. It's you, as a person. It's not something a woman has to prove by spending so many hours in a day doing housework. If a woman like Alice chooses to center her life around her home, that's great—for her. Because she wants to do that, not because some artificial cultural standard says she must. For if she is *forced* by her society to play that role, she will resent it and will largely fail at it.

However, as women are beginning to fulfill more unique, different roles in this society, there are some special needs which arise. With greater freedom comes an awareness of feelings and questions and thus the need to communicate more. Not long ago a national television station portrayed this need in "Tell Me Where It Hurts." In this poignant, beautifully executed drama a group of women are portrayed who appear ordinary enough on the outside but within themselves are feeling a desperate need to break out and express their personalities. As they begin to come out of their restricted existence the need to communicate with each other grows until, at the end, those who stayed with it emerge as much more whole people.

Increasingly I am amazed at how often a woman who sees me in my office may be expressing real feelings about her life for the first time. And with their expression comes a profound sense of relief, a relief which perhaps is based in really sharing yourself with another person and knowing that you are still accepted. John Powell in his book *why am i afraid to tell you who i am*? says: "But if I tell you who I am, you may not like who I am, and it is all that I have." That statement sums up many people's fears.

Madeline is in her late forties. She has one child upon whom she dotes and a very demanding husband who wants dinner at six and sex three times a week on schedule, whether she wants it or not. She can only have friendships of which he approves, which are not many, and she is not allowed to go many places without him. She cooks and bakes continuously and she is always at home for his noon-time telephone call. Madeline is a sweet, friendly, frightened nobody. She never complains but then again she doesn't appear all that happy. And once, just once, she broke down and cried because she couldn't stand her existence. She is unhappy but she's also too frightened and guilt-ridden to insist upon making some changes or even to talk about her problems. She's trapped—trapped in a sick marriage and in a role that is "what she's supposed to be because she's a woman." Extreme? a little. But real—and Madeline is not just one person—she's many.

Christians sometimes refer to Eve's sin in the Garden of Eden where she tempted Adam. Emphasis is placed upon her greater sin. But we sometimes forget that through Mary, a woman, the Son of God, the Redeemer, the King of Kings was brought into this world.

Women are in every sense of the word equal in worth to men. Yet they are vastly different. Balance lies in keeping both of those viewpoints in perspective to each other. The responsibility for this lies with every woman who realizes her uniqueness and worth and is therefore obligated to fulfill her life in the direction before God that is right for her.

L. G. Bachmann quotes the composer Anton Bruckner as saying to his friend:

"They want me to write differently. I could, too, but I may not. Out of thousands God in His mercy chose me and endowed me with talent, me of all persons. Some day I will have to account to Him. . ."

So must each woman—and each man—say of her own life, for we have each been born to our own unique role in life.